ESSAY ON THE BEAUTIFUL

PLOTINUS

Translated, with an introduction, by

THOMAS TAYLOR

THE ALEXANDRIAN PRESS

ISBN # 0-916411-86-9

INTRODUCTION

It may seem wonderful that language, which is the only method of conveying our conceptions, should, at the same time, be an hindrance to our advancement in philosophy; but the wonder ceases when we consider, that it is seldom studied as the vehicle of truth, but is too frequently esteemed for its own sake, independent of its connection with things. This observation is remarkably verified in the Greek language; which, as it is the only repository of ancient wisdom, has, unfortunately for us, been the means of concealing, in shameful obscurity, the most profound researches and the sublimest truths. That words, indeed, are not otherwise valuable than as subservient to things, must surely be acknowledged by every liberal mind, and will alone be disputed by him who has spent the prime of his life, and consumed the vigour of his understanding, in verbal criti-cisms and grammatical trifles. And, if this is the case, every lover of truth will only study a language for the purpose of procur-ing the wisdom it contains; and will doubt-less wish to make his native language the vehicle of it to others. For, since all truth is eternal, its nature can never be altered by transposition, though by this means its dress may be varied, and become less elegant and refined. Perhaps even this inconvenience may be remedied by sedulous cultivation; at least, the particular inability of some, ought not to discourage the well-meant endeavours of others. Whoever reads the lives of the ancient Heroes of Philosophy, must be convinced that they studied things more than words, and that Truth alone was the ultimate object of their search; and he who wishes to emulate their glory and parti-cipate their wisdom, will study their doctrines more than their language, and value the depth of their understandings far beyond the elegance of their composition. The native charms of Truth will ever be sufficient to allure the truly philosophic mind; and he who has once discovered her retreats will surely endeavour to fix a mark by which they may be detected by others.

But, though the mischief arising from the study of words is prodigious, we must not consider it as the only cause of darkening the splendours of Truth, and obstructing the free diffusion of her light. Different manners and philosophies have equally contributed to banish the goddess from our realms, and to render our eyes offended with her celestial light. Hence we must not wonder that, being indignant at the change, and perceiving the empire of ignorance rising to unbounded dominion, she has retired from the spreading darkness, and concealed herself in the tranquil and divinely lucid regions of mind. For we need but barely survey modern pursuits to be convinced how little they are connected with wisdom. Since, to describe the nature of some particular place, the form, situation and magnitude of a certain city; to trace the windings of a river to its source, or delineate the aspect of a pleasant mountain; to calculate the fineness of the silkworm's threads, and arrange the gaudy colours of butterflies; in short, to pursue matter through its infinite divisions, and wander in its dark labyrinths, is the employment of the philosophy in vogue. But surely the energies of intellect are more worthy our concern than the operations of sense; and the science of universals, permanent and fixed, must be superior to the knowledge of particulars, fleeting and frail. Where is a sensible object to be found, which abides for a moment the same; which is not either rising to perfection, or verging to decay; which is not mixed and confused with its contrary; whose flowing nature no resistance can stop, nor any art confine? Where is the chemist who, by the most accurate analyzation can arrive at the principles of bodies; or who, though he might be so lucky in his search as to detect the atoms of Democritus, could by this means give respite to mental investigation? For every atom, since endued with figure, must consist of parts, though indissolubly cemented together; and the immediate cause of this cement must be something incorporeal or knowledge can have no stability and enquiry no end. Where, says Mr Harris, is the microscope which can discern what is smallest in nature? Where the telescope which can see at what point in the universe wisdom first began? Since, then, there is no portion of matter which may not be the subject of experiments without end, let us betake ourselves to the regions of mind, where all things are bounded in intellectual measure; where everything is permanent and beautiful, eternal and divine. Let us quit the study of particulars, for that which is general and comprehensive, and through this, learn to see and recognize whatever exists.

With a view to this desirable end, I have presented the reader with a specimen of that sublime wisdom which first arose in the colleges of the Egyptian priests, and flourished afterwards in Greece; which was there cultivated by Pythagoras, under the mysterious veil of numbers; by Plato, in the graceful dress of poetry; and was systematized by Aristotle, as far as it could be reduced into scientific order; which, after becoming in a manner extinct, shone again with its pristine splendour among the philosophers of the Alexandrian school; was learnedly illustrated with Asiatic luxuriancy of style by Proclus; was divinely explained by Iamblichus: and profoundly delivered in the writings of Plotinus. Indeed, the works of this last philosopher are particularly valuable to all who desire to penetrate into the depths of this divine wisdom. From the exalted nature of his genius, he was called Intellect by his contemporaries, and is said to have composed his books under the influence of divine illumination. Porphyry relates, in his life, that he was four times united by an ineffable energy with the divinity; which, however such an account may be ridiculed in the present age, will be credited by everyone who has properly explored the profundity of his mind. The facility and vehemence of his composition was such, that when he had once conceived a subject, he wrote as from an internal pattern, without paying much attention to the orthography, or reviewing what he had written; for the celestial vigour of his intellect rendered him incapable of trifling concerns, and in this respect, inferior to common understandings, as the eagle, which in its bold flight pierces the clouds, skims the surface of the earth with less rapidity than the swallow. Indeed a minute attention to trifles is inconsistent with great genius of every kind, and it is on this account that retirement is so absolutely necessary to the discovery of truths of the first dignity and importance; for how is it possible to mix much with the world, without imbibing the false and puerile conceptions of the multitude; and without losing that true elevation of soul which comparatively despises every mortal concern? Plotinus, therefore, conscious of the incorrectness of his writings arising from the rapidity, exuberance and daring sublimity of his thoughts, committed their revision to his disciple Porphyry; who, though inferior in depth of thought to his master, was, on account of his extraordinary abilities, called by way of eminence the Philosopher.

The design of the following discourse is to bring us to the perception of the beautiful itself, even while connected with a corporeal nature, which must be the great end of all true philosophy and which Plotinus happily obtained. To a genius, indeed, truly modern, with whom the crucible and the air-pump are alone the standards of Truth, such an attempt must appear ridiculous in the extreme. With these, nothing is real but what the hand can grasp or the corporeal eye perceives, and nothing useful but what pampers the appetite or fills the purse; but unfortunately, their perceptions, like Homer's frail dreams, pass through the ivory gate; and are consequently empty and fallacious, and contain nothing belonging to the vigilant soul. To such as these a treatise on the beautiful cannot be addressed; since its object is too exalted to be approached by those engaged in the impurities of sense, and too bright to be seen by the eye accustomed to the obscurity of corporeal vision. But it is alone proper to him who is sensible that his soul is strongly marked with ruin by its union with body; who considers himself in the language of Empedocles, as

"Heaven's exile, straying from the orb of light";

and who so ardently longs for a return to his true country, that to him, as to Ulysses when fighting for Ithaca,

"Slow seems the fun to move, the hours to roll;
His native home deep-imag'd in his soul" (*note* 1).

But here it is requisite to observe that our ascent to this region of Beauty must be made by gradual advances, for, from our association with matter, it is impossible to pass directly, and without a medium, to such transcendent perfection; but we must proceed in a manner similar to those who pass from darkness to the brightest light, by advancing from places moderately enlightened, to such as are the most luminous of all. It is necessary therefore, that we should become very familiar with the most abstract contemplations; and that our intellectual eye should be strongly irradiated with the light of ideas which precedes the splendours of the beautiful itself, like the brightness which is seen on the summit of mountains previous to the rising of the sun. Nor ought it to seem strange, if it should be some time before even the liberal soul can recognize the beautiful progeny of intellect as its kindred and allies; for, from its union with body, it has drunk deep of the cup of oblivion, and all its energetic powers are stupefied by the intoxicating draught; so that the intelligible world, on its first appearance, is utterly unknown by us, and our recollection of its inhabitants entirely lost; and we become familiar to Ulysses on his first entrance into Ithaca, of whom Homer says,

> "Yet had his mind, thro' tedious absence lost
> The dear remembrance of his native coast" (*note 2*).

For,

> "Now all the land another prospect bore,
> Another port appeared, another shore,
> And long-continued ways, and winding floods
> And unknown mountains crowned with unknown woods":

until the goddess of wisdom purges our eyes from the mists of sense and says to each of us, as she did to Ulysses,

> "Now lift thy longing eyes, while I restore
> The pleasing prospect of thy native shore."

For then will

> " . . . . . the prospect clear,
> The mists disperse, and all the coast appear."

Let us then, humbly supplicate the irradiations of wisdom, and follow Plotinus as our divine guide to the beatific vision of the Beautiful itself; for in this alone can we find perfect repose, and repair those destructive clefts and chinks of the soul which its departure from the light of good, and its lapse into a corporeal nature, have introduced.

But before I conclude, I think it necessary to caution the reader not to mix any modern enthusiastic opinions with the doctrines contained in the following discourse; for there is not a greater difference between substance and shade than between ancient and modern enthusiasm. The object of the former was the highest good and supreme beauty; but that of the latter is nothing more than a phantom raised by bewildered imaginations, floating on the unstable ocean of opinion, the sport of the waves of prejudice and blown about by the breath of factious party. Like substance and shade, indeed they possess a similitude in outward appearance, but in reality they are perfect contraries; for the one fills the mind with solid and durable good, but the other with empty delusions; which like the ever‑running waters of the Danaïdes, glide away as fast as they enter, and leave nothing behind but the ruinous passages through which they flowed.

I only add, that the ensuing treatise is designed as a specimen (if it should meet with encouragement) of my intended mode or publishing all the works of Plotinus. The undertaking is, I am sensible, arduous in the extreme; and the disciples of wisdom are unfortunately few; but, as I desire no other reward of my labour, than to have the expence of printing defrayed, and to see Truth propagated in my native tongue; I hope those few will enable me to obtain the completion of my desires.

For then, to adopt the words of Ulysses,

> That view vouchsaf'd, let instant death surprise,
> With ever-during shaded these happy eyes!

BEAUTY,[4] for the most part, consists in objects of sight: but it is also received through the ears, by the skilful composition of words, and the consonant proportions of sounds; for in every species of harmony, beauty is to be found. And if we rise from sense into the regions of soul, we shall there perceive studies and offices, actions and habits, sciences and virtues, invested with a much larger portion of beauty. But whether there is, above these, a still higher beauty, will appear as we advance in its investigation. What is it then, which causes bodies to appear fair to the sight, sounds beautiful to the ear, and science and virtue lovely to the mind? Whether beauty is one and the same in all? Or whether the beauty of bodies is of one kind, and the beauty of souls of another? And again, what these are, if they are two? Or, what beauty is, if perfectly simple, and one?

For some things, as bodies, are doubtless beautiful, not from the natures of the subjects in which they reside, but rather by some kind of participation; but others again appear to be essentially beautiful, or beauties themselves; and such is the nature of virtue. For, with respect to the same bodies, they appear beautiful to one person, and the reverse of beauty to another; as if the essence of body were a thing different from the essence of beauty. In the first place then, what is that, which, by its presence, causes the beauty of bodies? Let us reflect, what most powerfully attacts the eyes of beholders, and seizes the spectator with rapturous delight; for if we can find what this is, we may perhaps use it as a ladder, enabling us to ascend into the region of beauty, and survey its immeasurable extent.

It is the general opinion that a certain commensuration of parts to each other, and to the whole, with the addition of colour, generates that beauty which is the object of sight; and that in the commensurate and the moderate alone the beauty of everything consists. But from such an opinion the compound only, and not the simple, can be beautiful, the single parts will have no peculiar beauty; and will only merit that appellation by conferring to the beauty of the whole.   But it is surely necessary that a lovely whole should consist of beautiful parts, for the fair can never rise out of the deformed. But from such a definition, it follows, that beautiful colours and the light of the sun, since they are simple and do not receive their beauty from commensuration, must be excluded the regions of beauty.   Besides, how, from such an hypothesis, can gold be beautiful? Or the glittering of night and the glorious spectacle of the stars? In like manner, the most simple musical sounds will be foreign from beauty, though in a song wholly beautiful every note must be beautiful, as necessary to the being of the whole. Again, since the same proportion remaining, the same face is to one person beautiful and to another the reverse, is it not necessary to call the beauty of the commensurate one kind of beauty and the commensuration another kind, and that the commensurate is fair by means of something else? But if transferring themselves to beautiful studies and fair discourses, they shall assign as the cause of beauty in these the proportion of measure, what is that which in beautiful sciences, laws or disciplines, is called commensurate proportion? Or in what manner can speculations themselves be called mutually commensurate? If it be said because of the inherent concord, we reply that there is a certain concord and consent in evil souls, a conformity of sentiment, in believing (as it is said) that temperance is folly and justice generous ignorance. It appears, therefore, that the beauty of the soul is every virtue, and this species of the beautiful possesses far greater reality than any of the superior we have mentioned. But after what manner in this is commensuration to be found? For it is neither like the symmetry in magnitude nor in numbers. And since the parts of the soul are many, in what proportion and synthesis, in what temperament of parts or concord of speculations, does beauty consist? Lastly, of what kind is the beauty of intellect itself, abstracted from every corporeal concern, and intimately conversing with itself alone?

We still, therefore, repeat the question, What is the beauty of bodies? It is something which at first view presents itself to sense, and which the soul familiarly apprehends and eagerly embraces, as if it were allied to itself. But when it meets with the deformed, it hastily starts from the view and retires abhorrent from its discordant nature. For since the soul in its proper state ranks according to the most excellent essence in the order of things, when it perceives any object related to itself, or the mere vestige of a relation, it congratulates itself on the pleasing event, and astonished with the striking resemblance (*note* 5) enters deep into its essence, and, by rousing its dormant powers, at length perfectly recollects its kindred and allies. What is the similitude then between the beauties of sense and that beauty which is divine? For if there be any similitude the respective objects must be similar. But after what manner are the two beautiful? For it is by participation of species that we call every sensible object beautiful. Thus, since everything void of form is by nature fitted for its reception, as far as it is destitute of reason and form it is base and separate from the divine reason, the great fountain of forms; and whatever is entirely remote from this immortal source is perfectly base and deformed (*note* 6). And such is matter, which by its nature is ever averse from the supervening irradiations of form. Whenever, therefore, form accedes, it conciliates in amicable unity the parts which are about to compose a whole; for being itself one it is not wonderful that the subject of its power should tend to unity, as far as the nature of a compound will admit. Hence beauty is established in multitude when the many is reduced into one, and in this case it communicates itself both to the parts and to the whole.) But when a particular one, composed from similar parts, is received it gives itself to the whole, without departing from the sameness and integrity of its nature. Thus at one and the same time it communicates itself to the whole building and its several parts; and at another time confines itself to a single stone, and then the first participation arises from the operations of art, but the second from the formation of nature. And hence body becomes beautiful through the communion supernally proceeding from divinity.

But the soul, by her innate power, than

which nothing more powerful, in judging its proper concerns, when another soul concurs in the decision, acknowledges the beauty of forms.   And, perhaps, its knowledge in this case arises from its accommodating its internal ray of beauty to form, and trusting to this in its judgment; in the same manner as a rule is employed in the decision of what is straight.   But how can that which is inherent in body, accord with that which is above body?   Let us reply by asking how the architect pronounces the building beautiful by accommodating the external structure to the fabric of his soul?   Perhaps, because the outward building, when entirely deprived of the stones, is no other than the intrinsic form, divided by the external mass of matter, but indivisibly existing, though appearing in the many.   When, therefore, sense beholds the form in bodies, at strife with matter, binding and vanquishing its contrary nature, and sees form gracefully shining forth in other forms, it collects together the scattered whole, and introduces it to itself, and to the indivisible form within; and renders it consonant, congruous and friendly to its own intimate form.   Thus, to the good man, virtue shining forth in youth is lovely because consonant to the true virtue which lies deep in the soul. But the simple beauty of colour arises, when light, which is something incorporeal, and reason and form entering the obscure involutions of matter, irradiates and forms its dark and formless nature. It is on this account that fire surpasses other bodies in beauty, because, compared with the other elements, it obtains the order of form; for it is more eminent than the rest, and is the most subtle of all, bordering, as it were, on an incorporeal nature. And too, that though impervious itself it is intimately received by others, for it imparts heat, but admits no cold. Hence it is the first nature which is ornamented with colour, and is the source of it to others; and on this account it beams forth exalted like some immaterial form. But when it cannot vanquish its subject, as participating but a slender light, it is no longer beautiful, because it does not receive the whole form of colour. Again, the music of the voice rouses the harmony latent in the soul, and opens her eye to the perception of beauty, existing in many the same. But it is the property of the harmony perceived by sense, to be measured by numbers, yet not in every proportion of number or voice; but in that alone which is obedient to the production, and conquest of its species. And this much for the beauties of sense, which, like images and shadows flowing into matter, adorn with spectacles of beauty its formless being, and strike the respective senses with wonder and delight.

But it is now time, leaving every object of sense far behind, to contemplate, by a certain ascent, a beauty of a much higher order; a beauty not visible to the corporeal eye, but alone manifest to the brighter eye of the soul, independent of all corporeal aid. However, since, without some previous perception of beauty it is impossible to express by words the beauties of sense, but we must remain in the state of the blind, so neither can we ever speak of the beauty of offices and sciences, and whatever is allied to these, if deprived of their intimate possession. Thus we shall never be able to tell of virtue's brightness, unless by looking inward we perceive the fair countenance of justice and temperance, and are convinced that neither the evening nor morning star are half so beautiful and bright.

But it is requisite to perceive objects of this kind by that eye by which the soul beholds such real beauties. Besides it is necessary that whoever perceives this species of beauty, should be seized with much greater delight, and more vehement admiration, than any corporeal beauty can excite; as now embracing beauty real and substantial. Such affections, I say, ought to be excited about true beauty, as admiration and sweet astonishment; desire also and love and a pleasant trepidation. For all souls, as I may say, are affected in this manner about invisible objects, but those the most who have the strongest propensity to their love; as it likewise happens about corporeal beauty; for all equally perceive beautiful corporeal forms, yet all are not equally excited, but lovers in the greatest degree.

But it may be allowable to interrogate those, who rise above sense, concerning the effects of love in this manner; of such we enquire, what do you suffer respecting fair studies, and beautiful manners, virtuous works, affections, and habits, and the beauty of souls? What do you experience on perceiving yourselves lovely within? After what manner are you roused as it were to a Bacchalian fury; striving to converse with yourselves, and collecting yourselves separate from the impediments of body? For thus are true lovers enraptured. But what is the cause of these wonderful effects. It is neither figure, nor colour, nor magnitude; but soul herself, fair through temperance, and not with the false gloss of colour, and bright with the splendours of virtue herself. And this you experience as often as you turn your eye inwards; or contemplate the amplitude of another soul; the just manners, the pure temperance; fortitude venerable by her noble countenance; and modesty and honesty walking with an intrepid step, and a tranquil and steady aspect; and what crowns the beauty of them all, constantly receiving the irradiations of a divine intellect.

In what respect then, shall we call these beautiful? For they are such as they appear, nor did ever anyone behold them, and not pronounce them realities. But as yet reason desires to know how they cause the loveliness of the soul; and what that grace is in every virtue which beams forth to view like light? Are you then willing we should assume the contrary part, and consider what in the soul appears deformed? for perhaps it will facilitate our search, if we can thus find what is base in the soul, and from whence it derives its original.

Let us suppose a soul deformed, to be one intemperate and unjust, filled with a multitude of desires, a prey to foolish hopes and vexed with idle fears; through its diminutive and avaricious nature the subject of envy; employed solely in thought of what is immoral and low, bound in the fetters of impure delights, living the life, whatever it may be, peculiar to the passion of body; and so totally merged in sensuality as to esteem the base pleasant, and the deformed beautiful and fair. But may we not say, that this baseness approaches the soul as an adventitious evil, under the pretext of adventitious beauty; which, with great detriment, renders it impure, and pollutes it with much depravity; so that it neither possesses true life, nor true sense, but is endued with a slender life through its mixture of evil, and this worn out by the continual depredations of death; no longer perceiving the objects of mental vision, nor permitted any more to dwell with itself, because ever hurried away to things obscure, external and low? Hence, becoming impure, and being on all sides snatched in the unceasing whirl of sensible forms, it is covered with corporeal stains, and wholly given to matter, contracts deeply its nature, loses all its original splendour, and almost changes its own species into that of another; just as the pristine beauty of the most lovely form would be destroyed by its total immersion in mire and clay. But the deformity of the first arises from inward filth, of its own contracting; of the second, from the accession of some foreign nature. If such a one then desires to recover his former beauty, it is necessary to cleanse the infected parts, and thus by a thorough purgation to resume his original form. Hence, then if we assert that the soul, by her mixture, confusion and commerce with body and matter, becomes thus base, our assertion will, I think, be right. For the baseness of the soul consists in not being pure and sincere. And as the gold is deformed by the adherence of earthly clods, which are no sooner removed than on a sudden the gold shines forth with its native purity; and then becomes beautiful when separated from natures foreign from its own, and when it is content with its own purity for the possession of beauty; so the soul, when separated from the sordid desires engendered by its too great immersion in body, and liberated from the dominion of every perturbation, can thus and thus only, blot out the base stains imbibed from its union with body; and thus becoming alone, will doubtless expel all the turpitude contracted from a nature so opposite to its own.

Indeed, as the ancient oracle declares, temperance and fortitude, prudence and every virtue, are certain purgatives of the soul; and hence the sacred mysteries prophesy obscurely, yet with truth, that the soul not purified lies in Tartarus, immersed in filth. Since the impure is, from his depravity, the friend of filth, as swine, from their sordid body, delight in mire alone.

For what else is true temperance than not to indulge in corporeal delights, but to fly from their connection, as things which are neither pure, nor the offspring of purity? And true fortitude is not to fear death; for death is nothing more than a certain separation of soul from body, and this he will not fear, who desires to be alone. Again, magnanimity is the contempt of every mortal concern; it is the wing by which we fly into the regions of intellect. And lastly, prudence is no other than intelligence, declining subordinate objects; and directing the eye of the soul to that which is immortal and divine. The soul, thus defined, becomes form and reason, is altogether incorporeal and intellectual, and wholly participates of that divine nature, which is the fountain of loveliness, and of whatever is allied to the beautiful and fair. Hence the soul reduced to intellect, becomes astonishingly beautiful; for as the lambent flame which appears detached from the burning wood, enlightens its dark and smoky parts, so intellect irradiates and adorns the inferior powers of the soul, which, without its aid, would be buried in the gloom of formless matter. But intellect, and whatever emanates from intellect, is not the foreign, but the proper ornament of the soul, for the being of the soul, when absorbed in intellect, is then alone real and true. It is, therefore, rightly said, that the beauty and good of the soul consists in her similitude to the Deity; for from hence flows all her beauty, and her allotment of a better being. But the beautiful itself is that which is called beings; and turpitude is of a different nature and participates more of non-entity than being.

But, perhaps, the good and the beautiful are the same, and must be investigated by one and the same process; and in like manner the base and the evil. And in the first rank we must place the beautiful, and consider it as the same with the good; from which immediately emanates intellect as beautiful. Next to this, we must consider the soul receiving its beauty from intellect, and every inferior beauty deriving its origin from the forming power of the soul, whether conversant in fair actions and offices, or sciences and arts. Lastly, bodies themselves participate of beauty from the soul, which, as something divine, and a portion of the beautiful itself, renders whatever it supervenes and subdues, beautiful as far as its natural capacity will admit.

Let us, therefore, re-ascend to the good itself, which every soul desires; and in which it can alone find perfect repose. For if any-one shall become acquainted with this source of beauty he will then know what I say, and after what manner he is beautiful. Indeed, whatever is desirable is a kind of good, since to this desire tends. But they alone pursue true good, who rise to intelligible beauty, and so far only tend to good itself; as far as they lay aside the deformed vestments of matter, with which they become connected in their descent. Just as those who penetrate into the holy retreats of sacred mysteries, are first purified and then divest themselves of their garments, until someone by such a process, having dismissed everything foreign from the God, by himself alone, beholds the solitary principle of the universe, sincere, simple and pure, from which all things depend, and to whose transcendent perfections the eyes of all intelligent natures are directed, as the proper cause of being, life and intelligence. With what ardent love, with what strong desire will he who enjoys this transporting vision be inflamed while vehemently affecting to become one with this supreme beauty! For this it is ordained, that he who does not yet perceive him, yet desires him as good, but he who enjoys the vision is enraptured with his beauty, and is equally filled with admiration and delight. Hence, such a one is agitated with a salutary astonishment; is affected with the highest and truest love; derides vehement affections and inferior loves, and despises the beauty which he once approved. Such, too, is the condition of those who, on perceiving the forms of gods or dæmons, no longer esteem the fairest of corporeal forms. What, then, must be the condition of that being, who beholds the beautiful itself?

In itself perfectly pure (*note* 7), not confined by any corporeal bond, neither existing in the heavens, nor in the earth, nor to be imaged by the most lovely form imagination can conceive; since these are all adventitious and mixed, and mere secondary beauties, proceeding from the beautiful itself. If, then, anyone should ever behold that which is the source of munificence to others, remaining in itself, while it communicates to all, and receiving nothing, because possessing an inexhaustible fulness; and should so abide in the intuition, as to become similar to his nature, what more of beauty can such a one desire? For such beauty, since it is supreme in dignity and excellence, cannot fail of rendering its votaries lovely and fair. Add too, that since the object of contest to souls is the highest beauty, we should strive for its acquisition with unabated ardour, lest we should be deserted of that blissful contemplation, which, whoever pursues in the right way, becomes blessed from the happy vision; and which he who does not obtain is unavoidably unhappy. For the miserable man is not he who neglects to pursue fair colours, and beautiful corporeal forms; who is deprived of power, and falls from dominion and empire but he alone who is destitute of this divine possession, for which the ample dominion of the earth and sea and the still more extended empire of the heavens, must be relinquished and forgot, if, despising and leaving these far behind, we ever intend to arrive at substantial felicity, by beholding the beautiful itself.

What measures, then, shall we adopt? What machine employ, or what reason consult by means of which we may contemplate this ineffable beauty; a beauty abiding in the most divine sanctuary without ever proceeding from its sacred retreats lest it should be beheld by the profane and vulgar eye? We must enter deep into ourselves, and, leaving behind the objects of corporeal sight, no longer look back after any of the accustomed spectacles of sense. For, it is necessary that whoever beholds this beauty, should withdraw his view from the fairest corporeal forms; and, convinced that these are nothing more than images, vestiges and shadows of beauty, should eagerly soar to the fair original from which they are derived. For he who rushes to these lower beauties, as if grasping realities, when they are only like beautiful images appearing in water, will, doubtless, like him in the fable, by stretching after the shadow, sink into the lake and disappear. For, by thus embracing and adhering to corporeal forms, he is precipitated, not so much in his body as in his soul, into profound and horrid darkness; and thus blind, like those in the infernal regions, converses only with plantoms, deprived of the perception of what is real and true. It is here, then, we may more truly exclaim, "Let us depart from hence, and fly to our father's delightful land" (*note* 8). But, by what leading stars shall we direct our flight, and by what means avoid the magic power of Circe, and the detaining charms of Calypso?" (*note* 9). For thus the fable of Ulysses obscurely signifies, which feigns him abiding an unwilling exile, though pleasant spectacles were continually presented to his sight; and everything was promised to invite his stay which can delight the senses, and captivate the heart. But our true country, like that of Ulysses, is from whence we came, and where our father lives. But where is the ship to be found by which we can accomplish our flight? For our feet are unequal to the task since they only take us from one part of the earth to another. May we not each of us say,

"What ships have I, what sailors to convey,
What oars to cut the long laborious way" (*note* 10).

But it is in vain that we prepare horses to draw our ships to transport us to our native land. On the contrary, neglecting all these, as unequal to the task, and excluding them entirely from our view, having now closed the corporeal eye (*note* 11), we must stir up and assume a purer eye within, which all men possess, but which is alone used by a few. What is it, then, this inward eye beholds? Indeed, suddenly raised to intellectual vision, it cannot perceive an object exceeding bright. The soul must therefore be first accustomed to contemplate fair studies and then beautiful works, not such as arise from the operations of art, but such as are the offspring of worthy men; and next to this it is necessary to view the soul, which is the parent of this lovely race. But you will ask, after what manner is this beauty of a worthy soul to be perceived? It is thus. Recall your thoughts inward, and if while contemplating yourself, you do not perceive yourself beautiful, imitate the statuary; who when he desires a beautiful statue cuts away what is superfluous, smooths and polishes what is rough, and never desists until he has given it all the beauty his art is able to effect. In this manner must you proceed, by lopping what is luxuriant, directing what is oblique, and, by purgation, illustrating what is obscure, and thus continue to polish and beautify your statue until the divine splendour of Virtue shines upon you, and Temperance seated in pure and holy majesty rises to your view. If you become thus purified residing in yourself, and having nothing any longer to impede this unity of mind, and no farther mixture to be found within, but perceiving your whole self to be a true light, and light alone; a light which though immense is not measured by any magnitude, nor limited by any circumscribing figure, but is everywhere immeasurable, as being greater than every measure, and more excellent than every quantity; if, perceiving yourself thus improved, and trusting solely to yourself, as no longer requiring a guide, fix now steadfastly your mental view, for with the intellectual eye alone can such immense beauty be perceived. But if your eye is yet infected with any sordid concern, and not thoroughly refined, while it is on the stretch to behold this most shining spectacle, it will be immediately darkened and incapable of intuition, though someone should declare the spectacle present, which it might be otherwise able to discern. For, it is here necessary that the perceiver and the thing perceived should be similar to each other before true vision can exist. Thus the sensitive eye can never be able to survey the orb of the sun, unless strongly endued with solar fire, and participating largely of the vivid ray. Everyone therefore must become divine, and of godlike beauty, before he can gaze upon a god and the beautiful itself. Thus proceeding in the right way of beauty he will first ascend into the region of intellect, contemplating every fair species, the beauty of which he will perceive to be no other than ideas themselves; for all things are beautiful by the supervening irradiations of these, because they are the offspring and essence of intellect. But that which is superior to these is no other than the fountain of good, everywhere widely diffusing around the streams of beauty, and hence in discourse called the beautiful itself because beauty is its immediate offspring. But if you accurately distinguish the intelligible objects you will call the beautiful the receptacle of ideas; but the good itself, which is superior, the fountain and principle of the beautiful; or, you may place the first beautiful and the good in the same principle, independent of the beauty which there subsists" (*note* 12).

Notes

(1) Pope's Homer's *Odyssey*, Book xiii., ver. 37.

(2) *Odyssey*, Book xiii., ver. 223.

(3) *Odyssey*, Book vii., ver. 303.

(4) It is necessary to inform the Platonical reader, that the Beautiful, in the present discourse, is considered according to its most general acceptation, as the same with the Good: though, according to a more accurate distinction, as Plotinus himself informs us, the Good is considered as the fountain and principle of the Beautiful. I think it likewise proper to observe, that as I have endeavoured, by my paraphrase, to render as much as possible the obscure parts evident, and to expand those sentences which are so very much contracted in the original, I shall be sparing of notes; for my design is not to accommodate the sublimest truths to the meanest understandings (as this would be a contemptible and useless prostitution), but to render them perspicuous to truly liberal and philosophic minds. My reasons for adopting this mode of paraphrase, may be seen in the preface to my translation of *Orpheus's Hymns*.

(5) "Enters deep into its essence," etc.
The Platonic Philosophy insists much on the
necessity of retiring into ourselves in order
to the discovery of truth ; and on this account
Socrates, in the first *Alcibiades*, says that the
soul entering into herself will contemplate
whatever exists and the divinity himself.
Upon which Proclus thus comments, with
his usual elegance and depth (in *Theol. Plat.*,
p. 7): "For the soul," says he, "contracting
herself wholly into a union with herself, and
into the centre of universal life, and remov-
ing the multitude and variety of all-various
powers, ascends into the highest place of
speculation, from whence she will survey the
nature of beings. For if she looks back upon
things posterior to her essence, she will
perceive nothing but the shadows and resem-
blances of beings ; but if she returns into
herself she will evolve her own essence, and
the reasons she contains. And at first indeed
she will, as it were, only behold herself ; but
when by her knowledge she penetrates more
profoundly in her investigations she will
find intellect seated in her essence and the
universal orders of beings ; but when she
advances into the more interior recesses of
herself, and as it were into the sanctuary of
the soul, she will be enabled to contemplate,
with her eyes closed to corporeal vision, the

genus of the gods and the unities of beings. For all things reside in us, after a manner correspondent to the nature of the soul; and on this account we are naturally enabled to know all things, by exciting our inherent powers and images of whatever exists."

(6) "And such is matter," etc. There is nothing affords more wonderful speculation than matter, which ranks as the last among the universality of things, and has the same relation to being as shade to substance. For, as in an ascending series of causes it is necessary to arrive at something, which is the first cause of all, and to which no perfection is wanting; so in a descending series of subjects, it is equally necessary we should stop at some general subject, the lowest in the order of things, and to which every perfection of being is denied. But let us hear the profound and admirable description which Plotinus gives us of matter (lib. vi., Ennead 3), and of which the following is a paraphrase: "Since matter," says he, "is neither soul, nor intellect, nor life, nor form, nor reason, nor bound, but a certain indefiniteness; nor yet capacity, for what can it produce? Since it is foreign from all these, it cannot merit the appellation of being, but is deservedly called non-entity. Nor yet is it non-entity in the manner as motion or station; but it

is true non-entity, the mere shadow and imagination of bulk and the desire of subsistence; abiding without station, of itself invisible, and avoiding the desire of him who wishes to perceive its nature. Hence, when no one perceives it, it is then in a manner present, but cannot be viewed by him who strives intently to behold it. Again, in itself contraries always appear, the small and the great, the less and the more, deficience and excess. So that it is a phantom, neither abiding nor yet able to fly away; capable of no one denomination and possessing no power from intellect, but constituted in the defect and shade, as it were, of all real being. Hence, too, in each of its vanishing appellations it eludes our search; for if we think of it as something great, it is in the meantime small; if as something more, it becomes less; and the apparent being which we meet with in its image is non-being, and as it were a flying mockery. So that the forms which appear in matter are merely ludicrous, shadows falling upon shadow, as in a mirror, where the position of a thing is different from its real situation; and which, though apparently full of forms, possesses nothing real and true—but imitations of being and semblances flowing about a formless semblance. They appear, indeed, to affect something in the subject matter, but in reality produce nothing; from their debile and flowing nature being endued with no solidity and no rebounding power. And since matter, likewise, has no solidity they penetrate it without division, like images in water, or as if anyone should fill a vacuum with forms."

(7) "In itself perfectly pure." This is analogous to the description of the beautiful in the latter part of Diotima's Speech in the *Banquet*; a speech which is surely unequalled, both for elegance of composition and sublimity of sentiment. Indeed, all the disciples of Plato are remarkable for nothing so much as their profound and exalted conceptions of the Deity; and he who can read the works of Plotinus and Proclus in particular, and afterwards pity the weakness and erroneousness of their opinions on this subject, may be fairly presumed to be himself equally an object of pity and contempt.

(8) "Let us depart," etc., *vide* Hom., *Iliad*, lib. ii., 140, et lib. ix., 27.

(9) Porphyry informs us in his excellent treatise, *De Antro Nymph*, "that it was the opinion of Numenius, the Pythagorean (to which he also assents), that the person of Ulysses in the *Odyssey*, represents to us a man, who passes in a regular manner, over

the dark and stormy sea of generation ; and thus, at length, arrives at that region where tempests and seas are unknown, and finds a nation who

> " Ne'er knew salt, or heard the billows roar."

Indeed, he who is conscious of the delusions of the present life and the enchantments of this material house, in which his soul is detained like Ulysses in the irriguous cavern of Calypso, will like him continually bewail his captivity, and inly pine for a return to his native country. Of such a one it may be said as of Ulysses (in the excellent and pathetic translation of Mr Pope) :

> " But sad Ulysses by himself apart
> Pour'd the big sorrows of his swelling heart,
> All on the lonely shore he sate to weep
> And roll'd his eyes around the restless deep
> Tow'rd the lov'd coast he roll'd his eyes in vain
> Till, dimmed with rising grief, they stream'd again." *

Such a one too, like Ulysses, will not always wish in vain for a passage over the dark ocean of a corporeal life, but by the assistance of Mercury, who may be considered as the emblem of reason, he will at length be enabled to quit the magic embraces of Calypso, the Goddess of Imagination, and to return again into the arms of Penelope, or

* *Odyssey*, book v., 103.

Philosophy, the long lost and proper object of his love.

(10) See Pope's Homer's *Odyssey*, book **v.**, 182.

(11) "We must stir up and assume a purer eye within." This inward eye is no other than intellect, which contains in its most inward recesses a certain ray of light, participated from the sun of Beauty and Good, by which the soul is enabled to behold and become united with her divinely solitary original. This divine ray, or, as Proclus calls it, mark or impression, is thus beautifully described by that philosopher (*Theol. Plat.*, p. 105): "The Author of the Universe," says he, "has planted in all beings impressions of his own perfect excellence, and through these he has placed all beings about himself, and is present with them in an ineffable manner, exempt from the universality of things. Hence, every being entering into the ineffable sanctuary of its own nature finds there a symbol of the Father of all. And by this mystical impression which corresponds to his nature they become united with their original, divesting themselves of their own essence and hastening to become his impression alone; and, through a desire of his unknown nature and of the fountain of good, to participate in him alone.

And when they have ascended as far as to this cause they enjoy perfect tranquillity and are conversant in the perception of his divine progeny and of the love which all things naturally possess, and goodness, unknown, ineffable, without participation and transcendently full."

(12) But before I take my leave of Plotinus, I cannot refrain from addressing a few words to the Platonical part of my readers. If such then is the wisdom contained in the works of this philosopher, as we may conclude from the present specimen, is it fit so divine a treasure should be concealed in shameful oblivion? With respect to true philosophy you must be sensible that all modern sects are in a state of barbarous ignorance; for Materialism and its attendant Sensuality have darkened the eyes of the *many* with the mists of error, and are continually strengthening their corporeal tie. And can anything more effectually dissipate this increasing gloom than discourses composed by so sublime a genius, pregnant with the most profound conceptions, and everywhere full of intellectual light? Can anything so thoroughly destroy the phantom of false enthusiasm as establishing the real object of the true? Let us then boldly enlist ourselves under the banners of Plotinus, and,

by his assistance, vigorously repel the encroachments of error, plunge her dominions into the abyss of forgetfulness, and disperse the darkness of her baneful night. For indeed there never was a period which required so much philosophic exertion, or such vehement contention from the lovers of Truth. On all sides nothing of philosophy remains but the name, and this is become the subject of the vilest prostitution; since it is not only engrossed by the naturalist, chemist, and anatomist, but is usurped by the mechanic in every trifling invention, and made subservient to the lucre of traffic and merchandise. There cannot surely be a greater proof of the degeneracy of the times than so unparalleled a degradation and so barbarous a perversion of terms. For the word philosophy, which implies the love of wisdom, is now become the ornament of folly. In the times of its inventor, and for many succeeding ages, it was expressive of modesty and worth; in our days it is the badge of impudence and vain pretensions. It was formerly the symbol of the profound contemplative genius, it is now the mark of the superficial and unthinking practitioner. It was once reverenced by kings and clothed in the robes of nobility; it is now (according to its true acceptation) abandoned and despised and ridiculed by the vilest plebeian. Permit me, then, my friends, to address you in the words of Achilles to Hector:

> " Rouse, then, your forces this important hour,
>   Collect your strength and call forth all your pow'r."

Since, to adopt the animated language of Neptune to the Greeks,

> " . . . On dastards, dead to fame,
>   I waste no anger, for they feel no shame,
>   But you, the pride, the flower of all our host,
>   My heart weeps blood, to see your glory lost."

Nor deem the exhortation impertinent, and the danger groundless:

> " For lo ! the fated time, th' appointed shore,
>   Hark, the gates burst, the brazen barriers roar."

Impetuous ignorance is thundering at the bulwarks of philosophy and her sacred retreats are in danger of being demolished, through our feeble resistance. Rise then, my friends, and the victory will be ours. The foe is indeed numerous, but at the same time feeble; and the weapons of truth in the hands of vigorous union, descend with irresistible force, and are fatal wherever they fall.